T0147179

Reconciliator

John 1:6-8 There was a man sent from God, whose name was _____
The same came for a witness, to bear witness of the Light, that all men through Him might believe. He was not that Light, but was sent to bear witness of that Light.

Lamb of GOD who takes away
the sins of the World

By atonement alone
man enters HIS presence
HE only is our atonement
And I, if I be lifted up from the
earth, will draw all men unto
me. (John 12:32)

The Icing on the Cake

PIXIE HOWSON

WESTBOW
PRESS®
A DIVISION OF THOMAS NELSON
& ZONDERVAN

WestBow Press books may be ordered through booksellers or by contacting:

WestBow Press
A Division of Thomas Nelson & Zondervan
1663 Liberty Drive
Bloomington, IN 47403
www.westbowpress.com
844-714-3454

Scripture taken from the King James Version of the Bible.

ISBN: 978-1-6642-4839-7 (sc)
ISBN: 978-1-6642-4838-0 (e)

Library of Congress Control Number: 2021921974

Print information available on the last page.

WestBow Press rev. date: 1/20/2022

THE ICING ON THE CAKE

IS AS A WHITED SEPULCHRE
IS TO MAN– PURE AND CLEAN ON THE
OUTSIDE, SIN WELL HID WITHIN

The Icing On The Cake

The icing on the cake

Beautiful, pure and pristine,

Not at face value for truths sake

For whats outside is not whats within

Spirit being, in mortal land, whats at stake?

Eternal destination restored in Him

Buy one book, one for your next of kin

Battle cry Not one left behind"

Your kin and the Nation adopted by Him

50% of each purchase
propels Gods words to completion

North, South East and West
I will return them to their land
I will return them, I will return them"

And what He spoke, He brings about

THERE IS ONE OF OUR OWN IN HARMS WAY.

Presented To

....

From ....

He created the heavens.

And the whole world is in his hands.

To restore what was lost,
He sent his son.
His shed blood, his life the cost
To partake of him by confession,

Jesus I _____ am a sinner most cursed.

Of my sins there are a ton,
no strength I, by another I am undone.
Displace him Lord, in my life,
be the first one.

Vow to Fulfill

Jeremiah 32:37
Behold, I will gather them from all the countries to which I drove them in my anger and my wrath and in great indignation. I will bring them back to this place, and I will make them dwell in safety.

Ezekiel 34:16
I will seek the lost, and I will bring back the strayed, and I will bind up the injured, and I will strengthen the weak, and the fat and the strong I will destroy. I will feed them in justice.

Isaiah 11:12
He will raise a signal for the nations and will assemble the banished of Israel, and gather the dispersed of Judah from the four corners of the earth.

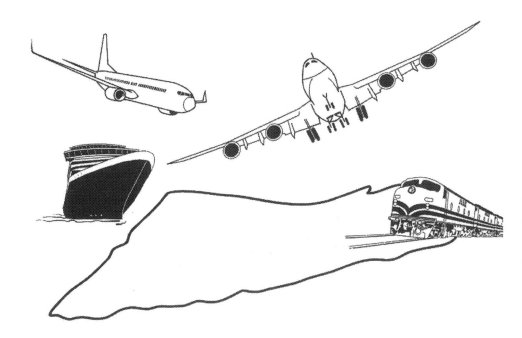

EZE 39: 27, 28, WHEN I HAVE BROUGHT THEM
AGAIN FROM THE PEOPLE, AND GATHERED THEM
FROM THEIR ENEMIES LANDS, AND AM SANCTIFIED
IN THEM IN THE SIGHT OF MANY NATIONS
THEN SHALL THEY KNOW THAT I AM THEIR GOD,
WHICH CAUSED THEM TO BE LED INTO CAPTIVITY
AMONG THE HEATHEN, BUT I HAVE GATHERED
THEM UNTO THEIR OWN LAND. NEITHER WILL
I HIDE MY FACE ANYMORE FROM THEM

First Adam

In the beginning God created the heavens in our time,
On the 6th day God created man,
Inbreathed His breath into the nostrils of him
Bequeathing man His spirit within
Oer the works of Gods hand man has dominion
Saying "eat not the fruit of the tree of knowledge and sin"
death will come as man strives for his own opinion
As man his God did disobey, God within man His spirit did slay
Saying to the temptor
"by the seed of the woman your crushed head shall pay"
Redemption to be by Davids line, the king to redeem mans dominion.

Fallen Man

Adam now fallen, glory abducted,
Man in rebirth, immortality corrupted
Propensity now for evil, enlarged his girth
Disease: instalments of death that sin inducted
Dominion now Satans, Man slave to his mirth
Atonement, His shed blood only the eternal adjustment

Second Adam

Where once Gods spirit was, a void now within,
Booze, pills, drugs sex; and pride of life fill in,
But nothing can quench that thirst within,
The Restored divine life, the cleansing of sin,
But to repent, receive divine life again
through the sent one, His Son;
Can the devils work be undone
Mortal to immortal, dominion regain
His shed blood to cleanse,
His word oer the land proclaim.

And the Lord
formed man,
a Triune being

SPIRIT
SOUL
BODY

Man's spirit is
forever, we decide
where that forever
will be.

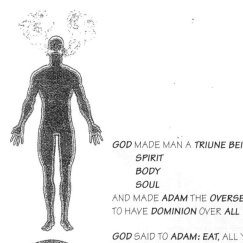

GOD MADE MAN A *TRIUNE BEING*
   SPIRIT
   BODY
   SOUL
AND MADE **ADAM** THE *OVERSEER*
TO HAVE **DOMINION** OVER **ALL**

GOD SAID TO **ADAM: EAT**, ALL YOU SEE IS *FOOD*
BUT *NOT* THE *TREE OF KNOWLEDGE*, ALL ELSE IS GOOD
EAT *NOT* OF THAT *TREE* FOR YOU SHALL *SURELY DIE*
WE **DESCENDED** FROM **ADAM**, DID **GOD** LIE?
MAN **LIVES**, YES **YOU** AND I,
WE ARE FOR SURE BOTH **ALIVE**
SO **HOW** IS THIS SO?
DID **GOD** LIE?

GOD DID NOT SURELY LIE
SO WHAT **THEN** DID **EXPIRE**?
THE **SPIRIT** OF **GOD** IN THE MAN HE MADE
MAN NOW **LOST** IN THE MIRE
FALLEN, DOMINION LOST TO THE ONE HE **OBEYED**
MAN **AWAITING** NEW BIRTH IN THE **SENT** ONE,
MESSIAH.

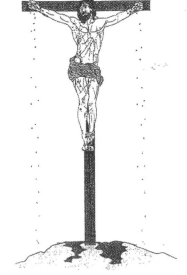

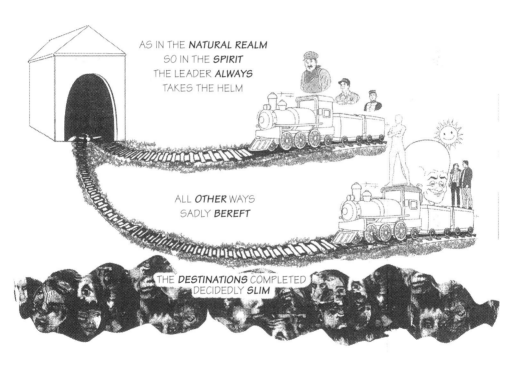

AS IN THE **NATURAL REALM**
SO IN THE **SPIRIT**
THE LEADER **ALWAYS**
TAKES THE HELM

ALL **OTHER** WAYS
SADLY **BEREFT**

THE **DESTINATIONS** COMPLETED
DECIDEDLY **SLIM**

THE *ENGINEER* AT THE *HEAD* OF THE *TRAIN* (*SPIRIT MAN*)

THE *GUARD* (THE *MIND*)

THE *PORTER* (THE *FLESH*)

Hierarchy

The
Wages of Sin

The wages of sin is death
That decreed is agreed upon
Your own rules, beliefs do not reality make.
Disputing gravity from the ninth floor
That "splotch" is not fake
Equally so, the eternal is true
selection is made this side of time by you
No direction, just destination lies past
Eternity's line
You will be with the Gods 'n idols that
you served here so fine
Or with the eternal living God
The creator divine
Is your soul's debt to be paid by God's gift
His son?
Or to be paid by the breaths of your
Expiring lung?
Eternally crying, "I will be as he,
Truth is mine!
Truth is mine!"
On the wrong side of eternity's line

ETERNITY'S LINE

HEAVEN   HELL

It is the most precious gift we have, by free will, we are 'moral being'
Neither saint nor murderer so born, but by act of will, we become
The architect of life by acts of will, each one

IN ANCIENT **TRAILS...**
TRUTH PREVAILS
THE **TRUTH** THAT THEY **FOLLOW** WILL PASS MANY A **SCENE**

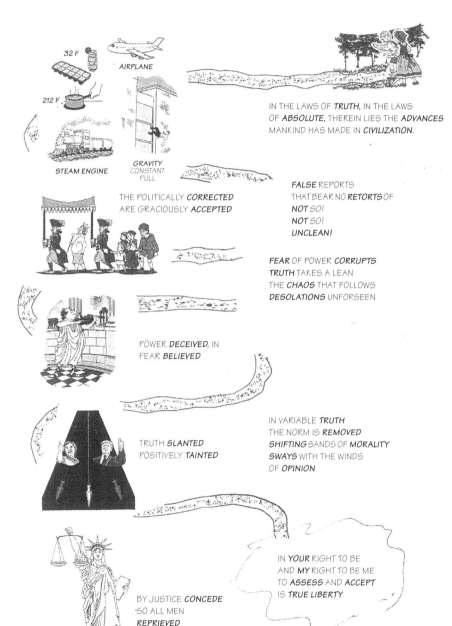

32 F

AIRPLANE

212 F

STEAM ENGINE

GRAVITY
CONSTANT
PULL

IN THE LAWS OF **TRUTH**, IN THE LAWS
OF **ABSOLUTE**, THEREIN LIES THE **ADVANCES**
MANKIND HAS MADE IN **CIVILIZATION**.

THE POLITICALLY **CORRECTED**
ARE GRACIOUSLY **ACCEPTED**

FALSE REPORTS
THAT BEAR NO **RETORTS** OF
NOT SO!
NOT SO!
UNCLEAN!

FEAR OF POWER **CORRUPTS**
TRUTH TAKES A LEAN
THE **CHAOS** THAT FOLLOWS
DESOLATIONS UNFORSEEN

POWER **DECEIVED**, IN
FEAR **BELIEVED**

TRUTH **SLANTED**
POSITIVELY **TAINTED**

IN VARIABLE **TRUTH**
THE NORM IS **REMOVED**
SHIFTING SANDS OF **MORALITY**
SWAYS WITH THE WINDS
OF **OPINION**

BY JUSTICE **CONCEDE**
SO ALL MEN
REPRIEVED

IN **YOUR** RIGHT TO BE
AND **MY** RIGHT TO BE ME
TO **ASSESS** AND **ACCEPT**
IS **TRUE LIBERTY**

THE ICING ON THE CAKE

Is as a whited sepulchre is to man-pure
and clean on the outside the truth
of sin well hid within.

What on earth is going on?
Where're all the people gone?
What ending? Is there one past trending?

It's on earth the making of eternal staking
man to follow His soul's rending
Where're they gone, message sending,
message sending...

As the icing covers
identical cakes, what hides
within, one cake vanilla, the
other the dark color of sin.

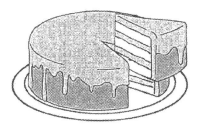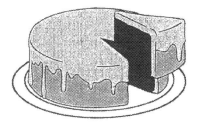

THE **ICING ON** THE CAKE

IS AS A **WHITED SEPULCHRE** IS TO MAN.

PURE AND CLEAN **OUTSIDE**

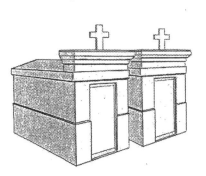

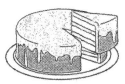

THE **TRUTH** WELL HID **WITHIN.**

AS **KNOWLEDGE** OF **NATURAL LAW ADVANCES** MAN...

...**SO** IN THE **SPIRITUAL,** IN THE **ABSOLUTE LAWS** OF **TRUTH,** MAN FINDS **"I AM"** IN HIS **SEARCH** FOR **WHO AM I?**

35 F

212 F

STEAM ENGINE

AIRPLANE

SPACE SHUTTLE

GRAVITY CONSTANT PULL

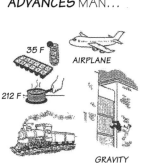

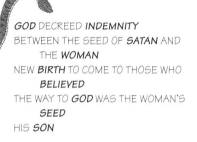

GOD DECREED INDEMNITY
BETWEEN THE SEED OF SATAN AND
    THE WOMAN
NEW BIRTH TO COME TO THOSE WHO
    BELIEVED
THE WAY TO GOD WAS THE WOMAN'S
    SEED
HIS SON

IN APPEARANCE THE FALLEN AND NEW MAN THE SAME
EVEN TO SAY I BELIEVE, I'M CHURCHED,
I'M GOOD AND KIND
BUT GOD SEEKS NOT THE RIGHTEOUSNESS
OF MAN
FOR REDEMPTION FROM SIN, HE GAVE
THE BLOOD OF HIS SON

APPEARANCES ARE TO MAN OF GREAT IMPORT
WHITED SEPULCHERS WITHOUT BUT THE SHADE
OF HIS OWN GOD WITHIN
EXTERNAL DEEDS OF RIGHTEOUSNESS,
EACH TO HIS OWN GOD MEN TAUGHT
BUT GOD PLACED HIS SON IN THE DOORWAY TO HIM
BY NO DEEDS OF CHARITY AND GOODNESS
CAN A SPOT IN HEAVEN BE BOUGHT,
GOD PLACED HIS SON ONLY TO BE THE DOORWAY
IN THE BLOOD OF THE LAMB ONLY LIES THE
WASHING OF SIN.

22

The Copyright.

The King as in Elvis.
By man long revered
Royalties his legacy gets all monies received
So creation in thought
In structure, art or design
Protected by decree of Copy right "its mine!"
All glory due to he,
Ownership inherent to the one of creation,
Creative intelligence precious, protected by command.

With copyright laws that rule every land
So man protects intellectual rights in the natural
But strangely denies the same rights eternal
Thecreators laws made to maintain optimum design
plagiarized by mans religions,
Other gods not devine
The mountains, hills, valleys, the oceans, the oceans moon and tide
The nature he created worshipped,
The creator denied

From Lucifer to spirit of plants, from witchcraft spells, mans pride
All these works of woods and straw to burn.
Deception by he who first lied.
Man, each to his own way, his own god
Not by the cross of His Son
To be eternally with the Creator Divine,
His copyright, God decreed, is through the doorway of His Son

Who's fairy tale shall you believe?

Lady Bird Lady Bird fly away home
Your house is on fire your children are gone
You might look like your in transition
Your dots sign of change to come
But believe me your complete
You won't be another someone
The theory of evolution still a theory not proven sum
Of all the worlds species no transitionary evidence found, nary a one
Not one halfway fossil, no species half done
If evolution be true there'd not be one, but a ton
And "all of this creation" comes from a vacuum?
Where none plus none makes none?
Great faith indeed for transition than creation
Where random dust becomes the precision timed world we live in?
Intelligent design better answers this creative reign
Its absolutely in truth the foundations of mans civilized gain
So fly away lady bird fly away home
Your house is on fire
Your children are gone

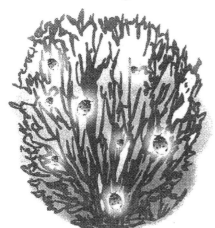

Man On A Peacock

Primal genetic intent denied, I am not so wired
And again, be as God I aspired, by hormone injection, knifed organ transformation
Is mans hand to creation, to thwart Gods intention
By knowledge of deception, the same willful malfunction
When married, in another, find consummation, or while not wed, release in fornication,
Or wrongfully "loving" those under aged in protection, or eyes on anothers fine things of collection
One stoops to unlawful appropriation, to break our laws of stabilization
By pride, that all consuming core of selfish consumption, anarchy reigns, down civilization,
There is a black hole inside of me, just like the ones in the galaxy
All matter I must feed upon, light gone black hole centred unto death
Feed me! Feed me! Where is my liberty, to free me?
There is a black hole inside of me, Feed me! Feed me!

Proud as a peacock he sat, But let God not be denied
Or the Son He did begat, Sins core, mans pride, God denied
Base appetites multiplied, For pride "the black hole" inside

THE PAGANS IDOL
IN *HIS* PRESENCE DID FALL
BROKEN IN TWO
AS THE NIGHT DID *FALL*
MAN MADE IDOLS MADE AND FIXED
BY *ME* AND YOU ALL
'NO GRAVEN IMAGE' *ETERNAL* COMMAND!
IN THE ARK OF *HIS PRESENCE*
NO IDOL SHALL STAND
HE CHANGES NOT TOWARD SUCH OFFENCE
ETERNAL ATONEMENT *HIS* SHED *BLOOD* DEMAND
IN *HIS* GODHEAD NO MANS MUTATION SHALL STAND

ISAIAH 57:13 PAGANS OF OLD WORSHIPED IDOLS USING SMOOTH STONES IN STREAMS

ALTAR

DAVID PICKED UP 5 SMOOTH STONES TO FIGHT THE PAGAN WHO CHALLENGED THE ARMIES OF GOD ALMIGHTY. THE SOURCE OF HIS DEATH WAS THAT WHICH THE PAGAN WORSHIPPED

DIVINE DIRECTION GOD'S PROTECTION THE AIM IS GOD'S THE HIT IS GOD'S HE IS LOOKING FOR 'DAVIDS'

I HAVE FOUGHT A LION AND I HAVE FOUGHT A BEAR. WHO ARE YOU? YOU UNCIRCUMCISED PHILISTINE!

MEDIA
DECEPTION
LUST
SELFISHNESS
COVETNESS
LAWLESSNESS
SEXUAL SIN
DENIAL OF TRUTH FOR SIN

MAN TODAY ALSO WORSHIP IDOLS OF SMOOTH STONE

OUR IDOLS ARE INCLINED TO RELIGIONS
THAT INFLAME UNHOLY PASSIONS
MEN ARE LED TO ANY DEVIL
TO PURCHASE INDULGENCE FOR
SOME FAVORITE LUST
FOR SIN TO SELF ATONE
THOSE WHO FORSAKE THE ONLY RIGHT
WAY WANDER A THOUSAND BYPATHS
EACH ONE HIS OWN WAY
SERVING SIN, NOW ENSLAVED
ETERNAL CONSEQUENCE, EACH
TO THEIR OWN GOD ALONE.

SIGNS OF THE END TIMES

JOEL 3:1

"For behold, in those days and at that time,
when I restore the fortunes of Judah and Jerusalem,

ARAB COALITION

WORLD GOVERNMENT & UNITED NATIONS

WORLD BARTER CODE BUY & SELL

WORLD ARMED FORCES

KENITH COPELAND

THE ANTI-CHRIST

ONE WORLD RELIGION

WORLD BANK

ISRAEL

Jerusalem

MATTHEW 16:3

JESUS SAID "WHEN *EVENING* COMES, YOU SAY; "THE *WEATHER* WILL BE *FOUL*, FOR THE SKY IS *RED* AND IN THE MORNING. TODAY IT WILL BE *STEAMY*, FOR THE *SKY* IS *RED* AND *OVERCAST*. A *WICKED* AND *ADULTEROUS* GENERATION DEMANDS A *SIGN*. YOU *HYPOCRITES!* YOU KNOW HOW TO INTERPRET THE *APPEARANCE* OF THE *EARTH* AND SKY. *WHY* DON'T YOU KNOW HOW TO *INTERPRET* THE PRESENT *TIME?*

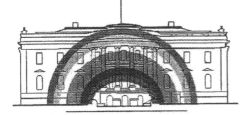

Matt. 16:2

When evening comes, you say,
The weather will be fair, for the sky is red,
and in the morning, Today it will be stormy,
for the sky is red and overcast.
You know how to interpret
the appearance of the sky,
but not the signs of the times!

WHEN **TRUTH** DIES
VIRTUAL REALITY ONCE **FALSE**, NOW **TRUE**
ALL **REASON** FLIES
DEATH OF CULTURE **ENSUE**
EMPIRES **DIE** NOT **WITHOUT** BUT **WITHIN**
REFERENCE POINTS GONE
MAN'S THOUGHTS **PATHOGEN**
TOO LATE, WE REALISE **ETERNITY** IS
NOT THE TIME WE **LIVED** IN
BUT HOW WE **SERVED** HERE
FITS US WHERE WE WILL BE
OUR **PERFECT** SLOT FOR **ETERNITY**
WITH THE **CREATOR DIVINE**
OR THE **DECEIVER** IN **SIN**

35

Are you a Couch Potato?
The couch potato is a man who excercises prone on his couch
States as a runner I'm no slouch
Just as a couch potato to athletic form can't claim
Because he can walk does not make olympian fame
So religions that claim Christian but deny Jesus His name,
From "the way" He came to show, they refrain,
Going each their own way, saying "all ways are the same".
Political correctness allows all, its this worlds game
No thought wicked, no act cause pain
That is why God sent His Son to guide you to His reign,
By truth, not delusion and collusion
That increases hells gain.

"ABRAHAM *STOP!* AND THERE
IN THE THICKET WAS A *RAM,*
ON THE MOUNT OF THE *LORD,*
GOD PROVIDES THE SACRIFICE"

- THE WORD OF *GOD* EMPOWERS
- *GOD* PROVIDES THE *SACRIFICE*
- MAN PROVIDES THE *OBEDIENCE*

GOD'S SACRIFICE FOR SIN UPON HIS MOUNT
FORGED IN *OBEDIENCE,* MADE *PERFECT,* HIS *SON*
ETERNAL SPIRIT, IN THE *FLESH,* DID *SIN* OVERCOME
JESUS CHRIST CRUCIFIED, *HIS* BLOOD *SIN ATONE*
IF WE CONFESS SIN *HE* IS FAITHFUL AND JUST TO *FORGIVE,*
OVERCOME CAUSES US TO BE CLEANSED UNTO
RIGHTEOUSNESS TO BECOME ONE IN HIS *SON*
WHEN WE CONFESS *SIN,* THAT *"OLD MAN SPIRIT"*
IN US *DIES, HIS* LIFE IN US, RIGHT STANDING, DOES
RISE BECAUSE HIS FLESH WAS FIRST *CRUCIFIED*
BY *HIM* SPIRIT OF *"OLD MAN"* IN US *DIES*
WHEN WE *CONFESS* THE *SIN* FROM THE FATHER
OF *LIES,* SO WE IN *HIM,* BECOME *CRUCIFIED*
HIS FLESH *FIRST* TO SHOW THE *WAY*
WE IN *HIM* ENABLED, OUR DEBT *HE* DID PAY

JESUS KING OF JEWS
FOR *HIS* COUNTRYMEN SLAIN
ALSO RANSOM FOR *SOULS*
FOREIGN, 30 PIECES OF *SILVER*, THE
PRICE OF *SERVANT* NOW GONE
BECAUSE *HE'S DEVINE*, IN
THOSE WHO RECEIVE *HIM*
HE LIVES ON, *HE* LIVES ON!

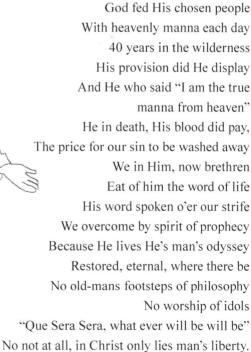

God fed His chosen people
With heavenly manna each day
40 years in the wilderness
His provision did He display
And He who said "I am the true
manna from heaven"
He in death, His blood did pay,
The price for our sin to be washed away
We in Him, now brethren
Eat of him the word of life
His word spoken o'er our strife
We overcome by spirit of prophecy
Because He lives He's man's odyssey
Restored, eternal, where there be
No old-mans footsteps of philosophy
No worship of idols
"Que Sera Sera, what ever will be will be"
No not at all, in Christ only lies man's liberty.

Psalm 147:15, 16, 17
He sends forth His commandment upon the earth
His word runneth very swiftly
He give the snow like wool:
He scattereth the hoarfrost like ashes,
He casteth forth His ice like morsels:
Who can stand before His cold?
He sendeth out His word, And melteth them:
He causes His wind to blow,
And the waters flow.

PEACE BE STILL
JESUS CALMED THE STORM
HIS WORD SPOKEN IN FAITH-
STILL CHANGES THE ATMOSPHERE

**DESOLATE DEAD
CITIES**
KINGDOMS UNDER RULE

ISAIAH 42:
V13 THE LORD SHALL GO
FORTH AS A MIGHTY MAN
HE SHALL PREVAIL AGAINST
HIS ENEMIES

V14, I HAVE LONG TIME HOLDEN
MY PEACE
I HAVE BEEN STILL AND
REFRAINED MYSELF
NOW WILL I CRY LIKE A
TRAVAILING WOMAN

V16 I WILL BRING THE BLIND
BY A WAY THAT THEY KNEW NOT
I WILL MAKE DARKNESS LIGHT BEFORE
THEM, AND CROOKED THINGS STRAIGHT.
THESE THINGS WILL I DO UNTO THEM AND
NOT FORSAKE THEM

HEB 2:14 That
through death
he might destroy
him who had the
power of sin and
death.
That is the devil.

HEB 2:14
In as much then as
the children
partake of flesh
and blood
He also Himself
likewise took part
of the same

HEB 8:2
For the law of life
in Christ Jesus
has made me
free from the law
of sin and death

2 COR 5:17
Therefore if any
man be
In Christ, he Is a
new Creation, old
things pass away,
behold all things
are new

ROM 10:10
For with the heart
man.
Believes unto
Righteousness
And with the mouth
Confession is made
Unto salvation

ROM 10:9
That if you confess
with Your mouth the
Lord Jesus and shall
believe in your heart
that God raised
Him from the dead
He shall be saved

JOHN 3:16
For God so loved
The world He gave
His only begotten
son. That whosoever
Believeth in Him
Should not perish
but have everlasting
life.

JOHN 3:3
Verily Verily
I say onto you
except a man be
born again he
cannot see the
kingdom of
heaven

Hail Mary, blessed among women,
When angels spoke Gods word
That she, Gods Son, shall conceive,
By grace, her faith, Gods word believed,
By which, her saviour brought all men reprieve,
Man fallen in original sin,
Cleansed all who received His sons life, from within,
For man, new birth, redeemed from sin,
By virgin birth, Emmanuel, mans new life begin.

Suffer little children, to come unto me.

The Great Exchange

No man takes my life. My father shows me how.

To lay down my life

and how to pick it up again

I would have lost all hope

if I had not believed

I would see the goodness of God

in the land of the living

After 3 days I rose again

Because I live

Because I did hope

Because in all those that believe in me

They abide in me

Greater is he who lives in me

By my word they abide in me

Former things come to pass. Now I declare new things before they spring forth, I will proclaim them to you.

…before today you have not heard them. So that you will not say, "Behold I knew them."

they that believe in me live
they that believe in me,
I am their hope
I shall pick up my life again

and I abide in them
not he of this world

and I in them. His power strength and might he bequeaths to those who believe.

Behold I will do something new, now it shall spring forth. I will even make a roadway in the wilderness.

Call to me and I will answer you and I will tell you great and mighty things.

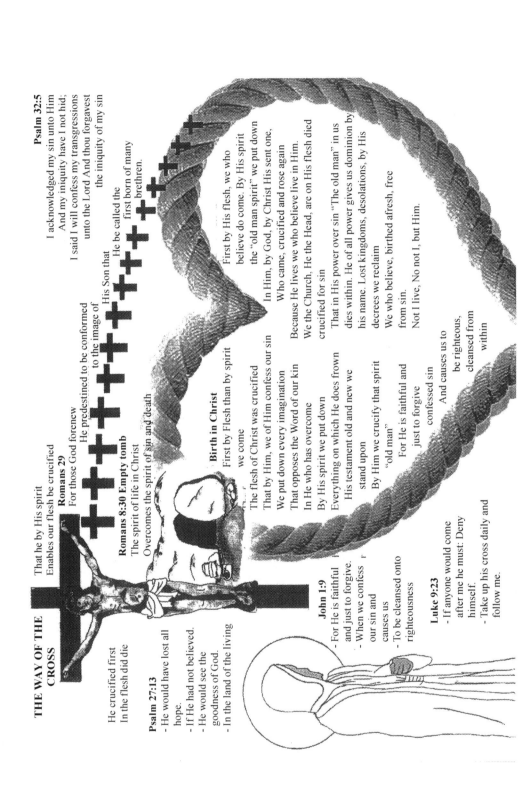

THE WAY OF THE CROSS

That he by His spirit
Enables our flesh be crucified

Romans 29
For those God forenew
He predestined to be conformed
to the image of
His Son that
He be called the
first born of many
brethren.

Psalm 32:5
I acknowledged my sin unto Him
And my iniquity have I not hid;
I said I will confess my transgressions
unto the Lord And thou forgavest
the iniquity of my sin

He crucified first
In the flesh did die

Psalm 27:13
- He would have lost all hope.
- If He had not believed.
- He would see the goodness of God.
- In the land of the living

Romans 8:30 Empty tomb
The spirit of life in Christ
Overcomes the spirit of sin and death

Birth in Christ
First by Flesh than by spirit
we come
The flesh of Christ was crucified
That by Him, we of Him confess our sin
We put down every imagination
That opposes the Word of our kin
In He who has overcome
By His spirit we put down
Everything on which He does frown
His testament old and new we
stand upon
By Him we crucify that spirit
"old man"
For He is faithful and
just to forgive
confessed sin
And causes us to
be righteous,
cleansed from
within

First by His flesh, we who
believe do come. By His spirit
the "old man spirit" we put down
In Him, by God, by Christ His sent one,
Who came, crucified and rose again
Because He lives we who believe live in Him.
We the Church, He the Head, are on His flesh died
crucified for sin
That in His power over sin "The old man" in us
dies within. He of all power gives us dominion by
his name. Lost kingdoms, desolations, by His
decrees we reclaim
We who believe, birthed afresh, free
from sin.
Not I live, No not I, but Him.

John 1:9
- For He is faithful
and just to forgive.
- When we confess
our sin and
causes us
- To be cleansed onto
righteousness

Luke 9:23
- If anyone would come
after me he must: Deny
himself.
- Take up his cross daily and
follow me.

The time of your visitation

is now

In the beginning…
and the world was
dark and void

Holy Spirit
hovered over the earth.

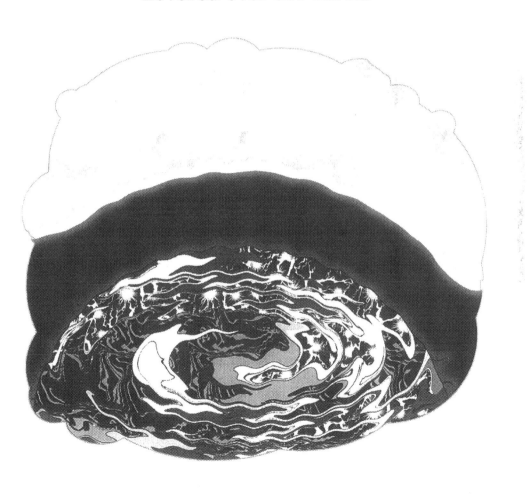

God Spoke

"Let there be light."

IN THE **BEGINNING**...
THE **LIGHT** SHINES
IN **DARKNESS**.

HIS LIFE **SHEATHED** IN THE **WORD** OF **HIS** POWER
AND THE **LIGHT** BELONGS IN THE **DARKNESS**.
FOR **LIFE** IN A **DARK** WORLD SPOKE **HE** FORTH HIS **WORD**.
AS THEN, SO NOW, **HIS** WORD **SPOKEN**,
BRINGS FORTH HIS **LIGHT**.

**And the Lord
put Adam into
the Garden of Eden.**

God gave man dominion
over his works.

In giving man self will,
God made man
a moral agent.

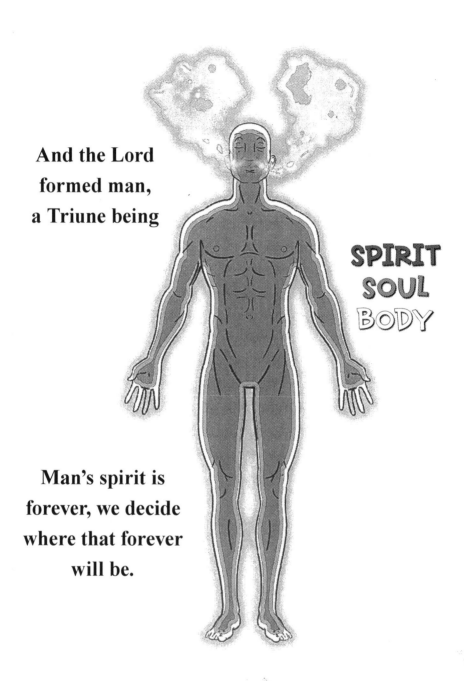

And the Lord formed man, a Triune being

SPIRIT
SOUL
BODY

Man's spirit is forever, we decide where that forever will be.

**Saying to man, eat all you want
freely, but do not eat of the
fruit of the tree of knowledge
of good and evil.**

HAS **GOD** SAID YOU SHALL
NOT EAT OF EVERY **TREE**
YOU SHALL **SURELY**
NOT DIE

FOR **GOD** DOES
KNOW THE DAY THAT
YOU **EAT**

YOUR **EYES** WILL
BE **OPENED**

YOU **SHALL** BE AS **GOD**
KNOWING **GOOD** AND **EVIL**

LUST OF EYE-
LUST OF FLESH
PRIDE OF LIFE
EVE SUBMITTED TO
TEMPTATION AND
DECEPTION. ADAM NOT
DECIEVED BUT A
WILLFUL ACT **LOST**
MAN'S **DOMINION OVER**
GOD'S WORKS,
TO THE **ONE** WHOM
HE **OBEYED**- HE GAVE DOMINION
TO THE **DECIEVER!**

-ADDING TO **GOD'S**
WORD OR TAKING
AWAY **CAUSES:**
-**CONFUSION**
-**DECEPTION**

-OUTRIGHT **DENIAL**
OF **GODS WORD.**
SUGGESTS
HIGHER WISDOM

-BE AS **GOD**

-OUTRIGHT **LIE**
AND **DECEPTION**
-MAN **DUPED** BY **LIE**

AND WHEN THE **WOMAN**
SAW THE **TREE** WAS **GOOD**
FOR FOOD AND THAT IT WAS
PLEASANT TO THE EYE
AND A **TREE** TO BE **DESIRED**
TO MAKE ONE **WISE**
SHE TOOK OF THE **FRUIT**
AND GAVE **ALSO** UNTO
HER **HUSBAND**

GOD SAID
"YOU SHALL **NOT EAT**
OF THE **TREE OF KNOWLEDGE,**
NOR SHALL YOU **TOUCH** IT,
"LEST YOU **DIE**".

**When man obeyed satan,
he became the slave
of he whom he obeyed.**

Man and creation
became fallen.

The fallen man operates
out of his selfish realm.

Sacrifice for the covering of sin.

God replaced Adam's cover of leaves with animal skin.

So... God showed Adam
removing his leaves,
by no act of man
can shame relieve

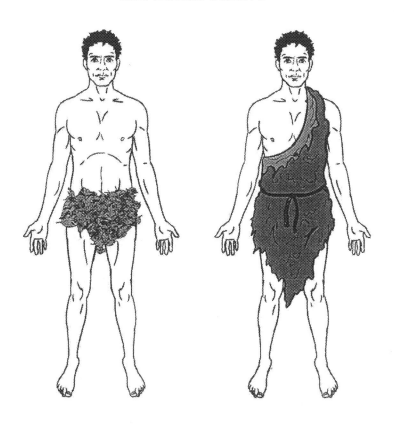

But in faith of the sacrifice he sent
In Christ we live, our sins repent
The price of sin in Him now paid
The new man now in Christ
is made.

God's work became satan's domain by Adam's submission.

Whomsoever you obey, becomes your master.

Fallen man and creation.

**Earth and man cursed-
labour for provisions.**

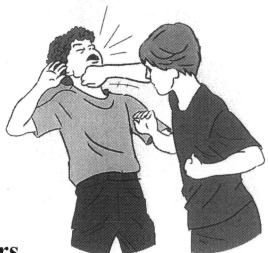

Sin enters the world.

Sin causes pain and suffering.

**Sin affects
others.**

Sickness is death by stages. Loss of peace, provision and health.

The penalty for sin is death.

And the Lord
formed man,
a Triune being

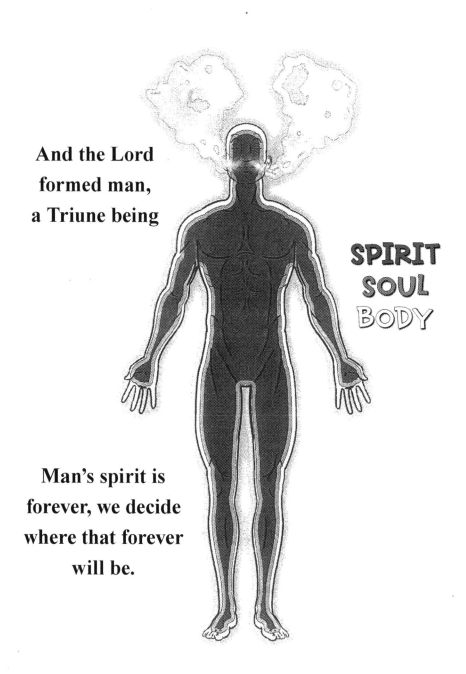

SPIRIT
SOUL
BODY

Man's spirit is
forever, we decide
where that forever
will be.

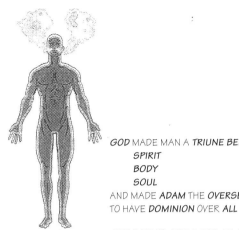

GOD MADE MAN A *TRIUNE BEING*
   SPIRIT
   BODY
   SOUL
AND MADE **ADAM** THE *OVERSEER*
TO HAVE *DOMINION* OVER **ALL**

GOD SAID TO **ADAM: EAT**, ALL YOU SEE IS **FOOD**
BUT **NOT** THE *TREE OF KNOWLEDGE*, ALL ELSE IS GOOD
EAT **NOT** OF THAT **TREE** FOR YOU SHALL *SURELY DIE*
WE **DESCENDED** FROM **ADAM**, DID **GOD** LIE?
MAN **LIVES**, YES **YOU** AND **I**,
WE ARE FOR SURE BOTH **ALIVE**
SO **HOW** IS THIS SO?
DID **GOD** LIE?

GOD DID NOT SURELY LIE
SO WHAT **THEN** DID **EXPIRE**?
THE **SPIRIT** OF **GOD** IN THE MAN HE MADE
MAN NOW **LOST** IN THE MIRE
FALLEN, DOMINION LOST TO THE ONE HE **OBEYED**
MAN **AWAITING** NEW BIRTH IN THE **SENT** ONE,
MESSIAH.

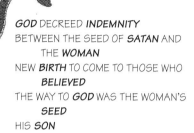

GOD DECREED **INDEMNITY**
BETWEEN THE SEED OF **SATAN** AND
    THE **WOMAN**
NEW **BIRTH** TO COME TO THOSE WHO
    BELIEVED
THE WAY TO **GOD** WAS THE WOMAN'S
    SEED
HIS **SON**

IN **APPEARANCE** THE **FALLEN** AND **NEW MAN** THE SAME
EVEN TO SAY I **BELIEVE**, I'M **CHURCHED**,
I'M **GOOD** AND **KIND**
BUT **GOD** SEEKS NOT THE **RIGHTEOUSNESS**
OF MAN
FOR **REDEMPTION** FROM **SIN**, HE GAVE
THE **BLOOD** OF HIS **SON**

APPEARANCES ARE TO MAN OF GREAT **IMPORT**
WHITED SEPULCHERS WITHOUT BUT THE SHADE
OF HIS OWN **GOD** WITHIN
EXTERNAL DEEDS OF **RIGHTEOUSNESS**,
EACH TO HIS OWN **GOD** MEN TAUGHT
BUT **GOD** PLACED HIS **SON** IN THE **DOORWAY** TO HIM
BY **NO** DEEDS OF **CHARITY** AND **GOODNESS**
CAN A SPOT IN **HEAVEN** BE BOUGHT,
GOD PLACED HIS **SON** ONLY TO BE THE **DOORWAY**
IN THE **BLOOD OF THE LAMB** ONLY LIES THE
WASHING OF SIN.

There is no forgiveness for sin without the shedding of blood.

First man is of God's breath inception
2nd man by God's word conception
To regain his life now fallen in sin
Receive by faith the blood sacrifice
His Son.

**Jesus bore our sin,
that we can be restored
to a sinless holy God.**

Isaiah 49:9
**I will preserve you and give you as a
covenant to the people to restore the earth.
To cause them to inherit the desolate heritages.**

Jesus comes to show the way.

In Him, man's dominion is restored. Jesus, the Son of God, brings heaven to earth through all that believe.

He is coming back for the lost are His that's why he came.

Isaiah 42:3
"He shall bring Forth Judgement unto truth"

We shut him out of our lives we put him in
LOCK OUT!
The things we treasured without Him were put in
LOCK OUT!

Government - Standstill

Health - on hold, beds to serve Covid 19

Police - serve complaints by phone call

Business's closed down - only essential business

Education - schools and universities closed

Entertainment closed, movie theatres, Restaurants, Sports closed

Families forced close quarters where
previously was busy and neglected

You worship idols and other gods
church buildings closed

He is coming back!

You lock me out!
I lock you down!
"A man reaps
what he sows"

And the Rainbow is His!

Ancestor of man

The descendant of Adam, the race of man
Inherits from his father original sin
God's breath in man, by disobedience did die
God's creation, now fallen, now ruled by he Who did lie
To wash clean that sin only shed blood can pry
God sent His son Jesus, His blood divine
Both looked alike, but "all now not mine"
To receive our Lord Jesus, that is the sign
The cross alone atones, makes all things Fine
For us to travel to God past eternities line

Drop of blood

Just: One drop of blood Lord
　　　My soul to refresh
Just: One drop of blood Lord
　　　A sinner's purchase
Just: One drop of blood Lord
　　　And I can go on
Just: Just one drop of blood Lord,
　　　My covenant bond
Just: One drop of blood Lord
　　　Your strength and not mine
Just: One one drop of blood Lord
　　　My lover divine
Just: One drop of blood Lord
　　　Sweet lover's caress
Just: One drop of blood Lord
　　　Eternal witness

You Came First

Thank you Lord that you came first
      And tread the treadmill alone
The cup of dregs you took for thirst
That my sins your blood atone

Thank you Lord for the cup you drank
Releasing chains of sin that bind
Because You came first, when this sea of
      of pain came I sank
Seeking death to end, found life instead
      In this Lord that I did find

This death that was mine because of
      Chains that do bind
Be it lust, pride of life, gods 'nother kind
His shed blood released me, deaths price
      paid, liberty, for me and all mankind

The road I now travel
I go not alone
Trials and all testing
With He who atones
His strength released
In the midst of my moans
The enemy defeated by
He who overcomes.

4 Day CONVENTION
TO BE HELD IN
LAHORE, PAKISTAN

Celebration 4 New Birthings

New Church

New Broadcasting Station

New Book Launch
"ICING ON THE CAKE"

New Denomination Birthed

"Last Days Church of JESUS CHRIST"
those birthed anew in JESUS CHRIST
John 10:9 I am the Door (the Church is NOT the door to the Christ ,
but Christ is the door to the Church)
Both Jew and Gentile (LDCOJC)
Mandate: To declare, decree and prophesy
and to fight speaking in tongues.

Printed in the United States
by Baker & Taylor Publisher Services